Sharing the Transition to College

Words of Advice for Diverse Learners and their Families

Jennifer Sullivan

Copyright © 2020 by Jennifer Sullivan.

Published by Tide Pool Books. All rights reserved. No part of this book may be used or reproduced in any manner whatsoever without written permission except in the case of brief quotations embodied in critical articles and reviews.

ISBN: 978-1-7355218-0-0

Printed in the United States of America

Book design by Cindy Samul

The names and incidents used in the examples are fictitious.
Any resemblance to actual persons or events is entirely coincidental.

Table of Contents

A Letter to Readers	7
Words of Advice for Students	11
Check the college's social media accounts	12
Show up for class a few minutes early	14
Communicate with your roommate	16
Be prepared for less privacy	18
Know the phone number of the Campus Safety office	20
The power of multiples – bring 1, 2, or 3	22
Be persistent	24
Explore assistive technology especially if you've never tried it before	26
Ask for help	28
Know the name and contact information of your Resident Assistants	30
Find the best place for you to do homework	34
Pick one day every week to do your laundry	36
Respect your roommate's space by keeping your belongings on your side of the dorm room	38

Even if you put in a lot of effort, college still might be hard	40
Find out where the health and counseling centers are located - even if you don't need them now	42
Keep a consistent sleep schedule	44
Keep important personal items in a drawer or out of sight	46
Write down usernames/passwords for your college email address, portal log-in, etc.	48
Personal hygiene - keep it private	50
Know when to contact your RA, Campus Safety, or call 911	52
Visit each professor at least once per semester in their office	56
Put yourself in social situations – even if it's uncomfortable	58
Know your learning style	60
Speaking up for yourself is impotant	62
Remember to keep your devices charged	64
Understand how your disability affects you	66
If you need accommodations, ask for them	68
Visit the Accessibility Office – it's a great resource	70
Be independent but don't be too proud to ask for help	72
Don't guess how well you're doing in your classes – find out	74

Words of Advice for Families — 77

- College is a marathon, not a sprint — 78
- Improve your student's executive functioning skills now — 80
- Only buy dorm room "essentials" that your student will use — 84
- Don't solve your student's problems until you ask THIS question first — 86
- Your student will bring their high school academic and social skills to college- for better or worse — 88
- Practice paying with a debit or credit card — 90
- Talk to your student about expectations for staying in touch with you — 92
- When your student calls with bad news, take care of them first; then take care of yourself — 94
- Your student will get sick while they are at college – it will be okay! — 96
- Expect your student to make mistakes — 98
- Make sure your student can make online purchases — 100
- Your first visit to campus may not meet your expectations — 102
- Attend the college-sponsored Family Weekend — 104
- Be patient. Your student will figure it out — 106
- Be prepared for a chaotic move-in day — 108
- Make organizational tools visible in your student's dorm room — 110

The accommodations process requires YOUR STUDENT to self-advocate	112
When your student comes home on breaks, have fun! Celebrate being with them!	114
Reinvest in yourself - devote time to your interests	116
Talk to your student about medications and refills	118
You will receive less communication about your student's progress in college than in high school	122
Give yourself time to adjust to your student being away at college	124
Ask about the support systems at your student's college	126
Colleges communicate with students, not parents	128
Help your student do what they don't want to do	130
Bonus Tip: Be prepared for an emotional rollercoaster ride when your student returns home from college on a break	132

A Letter to Readers

Congratulations! You are thinking about taking the next step in your educational journey – going to college! Deciding to attend college is the beginning of an exciting adventure! Whether you are a high school freshman, sophomore, junior or senior, or the parent of a high school student, you are probably feeling both excited and nervous about the transition from high school to college. This book was written to help you breeze through the transition.

The journey to college is a shared experience between a high school student and their family. The words of advice in this book will help students and families understand the emotional and physical journey of the other, which can strengthen the bond between a parent and child. Working through the book together can generate empathy, compassion, and understanding as you both share your feelings associated with the college transition.

Most books about going to college are written with just one audience in mind, either students OR families. This book is different; it offers tips and advice that both soon-to-be college students AND their families can share!

Included in this book are words of advice for often overlooked areas of college life like self-advocacy, student safety, dorm room organization, academic support, social life, and executive functioning. This book includes a wide variety of tips – many tips you will only find in this book! The words of advice are not listed in any particular order because all of the tips are important and it is difficult to say which advice is more important than another. So feel free to skip around and read the words of advice in any order you choose.

While the book is intended to be shared, how you choose to

explore the book is up to you. Students and families can read the book together, side by side, and talk about each tip and piece of advice; students can use the book in a classroom setting and discuss the tips with their teacher and peers; or parents can use the book for discussion with their spouse or other families. The book is a resource for whenever, and however, you need it. Read it together, or take turns. Read the sections for both students and families, or read the section that applies only to you. Again, the words of advice are not in a particular order so that you can read them in whatever order you choose. If you like, skip right to the tips that are most important to you at the moment. There is no wrong way to read this book.

It's important to note that each family's journey through the college transition will be different. Therefore, some tips may resonate with you more than others, and a tip that doesn't seem important now may become helpful sometime in the future.

At the end of most chapters is a short exercise for you to work on or a question for you to think about. Space is given for you to write down your responses if you find it helpful. Who knows – you may feel like shouting some of your responses from the rooftops, while it may feel better to provide other responses in silence. You may even want to share these tips with your college roommate, friends or other families who are going through the college transition too.

For Students: Relax, you've got this. This book offers tips and advice for your first year of college in ALL areas of your college life. If you are a high school student who plans to attend college, this is the perfect time to read, and start implementing, the tips in this book. Some of the tips offer advice for you to follow before you arrive on campus; some offer advice for move-in day; and some offer advice for your first days, weeks, and months on campus.

This book was inspired by the questions I am asked most frequently by new college students. I am passing along this valuable information to you – a soon-to-be college student – so that you will learn the secrets and strategies for a smooth transition to college.

For Families: Take a deep breath. You found a book that will help set your mind at ease about the college transition. How will YOU handle your student being away from home? How will YOU handle move-in day, and the moment you drive away from campus? What will YOU do if your student struggles during their first semester? If THESE are the types of questions that are on your mind, you will find comfort in the pages of this book.

The college transition is an emotional rollercoaster for you as well as your son or daughter, whether this is your first child leaving for college, or your second or third. Families feel all kinds of emotions, from excitement and pride for their college-bound student, to sadness and worry that their "baby" is leaving home. If your child has a learning, mental or physical disability your worries are increased, but you are probably feeling 'cautiously optimistic' about their transition to college.

Some families may be concerned about their child living on their own for the first time, while others may wonder if their child can handle the rigors of college academics. Some families may be uncertain about their child's ability to manage college life, like sleeping in a new place, sharing a small dorm room, waking up on time, doing their own laundry, making new friends, managing their medication, remembering to eat meals (or eating too many meals), attending classes, prioritizing homework over video games and parties, etc. I cover all these concerns, and much more, in this book.

Throughout my career as an educator, I have personally

counselled hundreds of families who were going through the college transition; those families had the same concerns you are having right now. Whether you are a student or parent, I am confident that you will find this book helpful and reassuring. I also believe this book will provide you with many "Aha!" or "I needed that" moments. If you have thoughts, concerns, or questions about your child's transition to college or about this book I would love to hear from you. Feel free to email me with your questions, feedback and stories of transition success! I also would love to know how this book was helpful to you in your college transition (as a student or parent). I am here for you! Please email me: **jsullivanauthor@gmail.com**

  I wish you the best of luck and much success in your college transition!

Jennifer Sullivan

Words of Advice
for Students

Student Tip #1

Check the college's social media accounts. (Twitter®, Instagram®, Facebook®, etc.)

Colleges and universities know that a complete college education includes making friends, socializing, and having fun – not just being successful in the classroom. Colleges want to keep you connected to the activities and events they host, so they utilize many forms of social media to advertise when and where events are happening. Before you arrive at your college, ask how you can connect to your school and what types of social media they use (Twitter®, Instagram®, YouTube®, Facebook®, etc.).

Colleges may have specific accounts/channels/feeds for different areas of student life, so connect with the ones you are most interested in – you don't need to follow every one. For example, you may want to know if Student Government has a Twitter account or if the Athletic Department has an Instagram account with pictures from recent games, or information about upcoming events. Each incoming class of students might have their own account or hashtag; this can be a great way to connect with other students before arriving at college. Extracurricular clubs/activities and even academic departments (such as Psychology, Hospitality, etc.) might have their own Instagram account. The point is that colleges and universities want you to join their activities. It's up to you to find out how your college/university promotes events. And it's up to YOU to stay informed and connected.

To Do

1. Go to your college website.

2. Find the Student Life or Campus Life section of the website.

3. Search for the ways that the college advertises and promotes student activities and events. Do they have an events calendar on their website? Do they use social media channels? If so, how many do they use?

List below the ways that the college advertises and promotes campus and student events:

Student Tip #2

Show up for class a few minutes early.

This is one of the most important tips for college-bound students. The start time of your class is exactly that – the time your class starts. Not a minute later. Arriving to class a few minutes early shows your professor that you think the class is important. Arriving a few minutes late implies that you don't care about the class. Even if you believe the class is important and have good intentions, but often arrive late, a professor who does not know you will only judge you based on your actions so don't be late! Some professors will even close and lock the classroom door immediately after class starts!

There are many strategies you can use to get to class on time. You can use your phone alarm to set reminders of your class time, set an alarm clock or use a voice-activated smart device in your dorm room to ensure you wake up on time, or walk to class with a friend holding each other accountable for being on time. Another strategy to help you be on time is to keep a copy of your class schedule in multiple places. For example, take a picture (or screenshot) of your schedule and keep it in your phone, hang a copy on a whiteboard in your dorm room, and put a copy in the front cover of your binders.

Real Life Scenario

Alex has an *Introduction to College Writing* class that starts at 10:00 a.m. on Mondays and Thursdays. Alex likes to shower and eat breakfast in the morning before class. It takes him 20 minutes to walk from his residence hall to the cafeteria on campus. Then it takes Alex 20 minutes to walk from the cafeteria to the academic building on campus where his class is held.

What time should Alex wake up in the morning to shower?

What time should Alex leave his residence hall to walk to the cafeteria for breakfast?

What time should Alex leave the cafeteria to be sure he arrives at his college writing class on time?

Student Tip #3

Communicate with your roommate. (Yes, this means you need to talk to them.)

During your first few weeks of college, your roommate is the person you'll spend the most time with. They will see you at your best and your worst. They will support you when you are stressed about your first college exam, and complain about your piles of clean and dirty clothes. You don't need to become best friends with your roommate, but you should build a relationship with them. By relationship, I mean you should become friendly with them. This is the person you'll be sleeping a few feet away from each night, and it will be very awkward if you and your roommate do not talk to each other.

Be prepared for some minor conflicts because anytime two people share space together there will likely be disagreements. I recommend having a conversation at the beginning of the semester to establish guidelines and rules for your room that you both agree upon. For example, who empties the trash, and when? Is it okay to invite guests into your room? Will you share food or will each of you buy your own snacks? Disagreements are expected because, well, you and your roommate are different people who grew up in different households with different rules and expectations.

So how will you handle these disagreements? Asking someone else (a friend, your parent, etc.) to talk to your roommate may help you avoid your roommate in the short term, but does not help you get along with them in the long run. If you find that you can't resolve your disagreements, or if little disagreements become big arguments, it's okay to ask a Resident Assistant to meet with both of you to help resolve the conflict. (More about Resident Assistants in Student Tip #10). Communication really is the best way to make friends and solve conflicts in college.

Real Life Scenario

Brandon and his roommate, Jay, get along pretty well. They keep their belongings on different sides of the dorm room, but share one mini-refrigerator. Brandon has noticed that his energy drinks are disappearing from the fridge. He assumes that Jay is drinking them and gets angry at Jay, but doesn't say anything. So Brandon eats Jay's chips to "pay him back". Jay notices that his chips are gone and gets angry at Brandon, but he doesn't say anything. When his friends come over to hang out, Jay tells them to eat Brandon's food because Brandon has been eating his chips.

What are 2 problems that you see in this scenario?

Why do you think Brandon and Jay are not talking to each other about why they are upset?

What could happen if the two roommates continue to avoid talking to each other about this situation?

How do you think an RA could help the two roommates solve this conflict?

Student Tip #4

Be prepared for less privacy.

If you choose to live in a residence hall on campus, you have a good chance of having a roommate – possibly two! Having more people in a room means less privacy for everyone. Sharing a room with another student means that two living spaces need to coexist, and all of the things that you do in your living space will be done side-by-side with another person nearby. For example, you will sleep a few feet away from your roommate, you will change clothes in the same room as your roommate, and your phone/FaceTime® conversations will be overheard by your roommate.

You and your roommate should talk about privacy, and what it takes for each of you to feel comfortable. Think about these questions: What time do you usually go to bed? Do you sleep in complete darkness, or do you like having a light on? When you change clothes or shower, do you use a bathrobe or an extra large towel? Do you have any mental health appointments using the computer or phone that require privacy?

Different people have different privacy needs. Different cultures also may have different expectations for privacy. It's important to know your roommate's privacy expectations when you share a room.

Think About It

What are your privacy needs? What rules does your family have about privacy in your house? If you are planning to share a room with a roommate in college, how could you start a conversation with that person about privacy? Write your thoughts below.

Student Tip #5

Know the phone number of the Campus Safety office.

When you are at college, it's very important to know who to call in case of an emergency. Every college and university has security officers who patrol the campus to make sure students and staff are safe. These officers are sometimes called Campus Safety officers or campus police. When you arrive on campus, be sure to ask for the phone number of the Campus Safety office and enter the number into your phone. Usually residence halls have this phone number posted on bulletin boards or scrolling TVs, but your Resident Assistant can give you the phone number as well.

Another way to get help in an emergency is to use the campus emergency phone system. Most colleges have emergency phones located outdoors around campus; they are brightly lit at night (usually with a blue light) and have an intercom call system. These phones will be connected to your Campus Safety office or the local 911 dispatcher.

Read more in Student Tip #20 to understand WHEN you should contact Campus Safety, your Resident Assistant, or call 911.

To Do

1. Go to your college website.

2. Search for the section on the website called Security, Campus Life, or Campus Safety.

3. Find 2 ways that the college keeps students safe. Write them below:

4. Find the Campus Safety phone number and write it below:

Student Tip #6

The power of multiples – bring 1, 2, or 3.

Phone and computer chargers are extremely important because they power your devices. Remembering to charge your devices is YOUR responsibility (we'll talk more about that later in Student Tip #25). Do not expect there to be charging outlets available in the classroom. Because charging cords are so important, you should bring more than one with you to college. Charging cords come in many different colors. I like white charging cords, but they blend into the color of most dorm room walls, and are easy to leave behind if you charge your devices in the campus library, dining hall, coffee shop, etc. I recommend buying brightly colored charging cords (such as green, blue, or pink), and bringing two or three charging cords for each of your devices to college. Use one charging cord every day in your dorm room, and keep the extra cords in a drawer or tote in your closet. Money saving tip: Buy these cords when they are on sale (i.e. back-to-school sales) and buy lots of them!

Students with executive functioning challenges (i.e. organization and memory challenges) may want to place two charging cords in their dorm room in highly visible locations (for example, next to their bed AND next to their desk). If the cords are placed in highly visible locations you will be more likely to see them and use them. If you want to use two cords in your dorm room, then I recommend buying at least two more cords to store and/or carry around with you (or keep for next semester). This same philosophy, the power of multiples, applies to other items that are important as well. Buy multiple hair brushes, tooth brushes, extension cords, etc.

Real Life Scenario

Jonathan brings his laptop to every class and, unfortunately, it's often not charged because he forgets to plug it in at his dorm room. He has one charging cord that is under his desk in his dorm room. When Jonathan is in class and his laptop isn't charged, he gets frustrated because he can't take notes.

What suggestion might help Jonathan remember to charge his laptop?

Student Tip #7

Be persistent.

You may experience setbacks and challenging times during your first year at college. Students who expect college to be easy will be in for a surprise! If you know there will be challenging times ahead, then you can prepare yourself, and build your personal toolbox. A personal toolbox can be full of tips, tools, and coping strategies that will help you when college gets difficult.

Persistence is one tool that absolutely needs to be in your personal toolbox. The definition of persistence is, "Firm continuance in the course of action in spite of difficulty or opposition." Continuing to work toward solving a problem, even when faced with difficulties, is one of the most important tips I can give you.

In college, you might encounter difficulty with an instructor, a roommate, a teammate, or a class. Instead of giving up when it's hard to keep going, college students need to ask for help (more in Student Tip #9). When things are tough, keep going.

Think About It

What does "being persistent" mean to you? Are there areas of your life/school where you have demonstrated persistence? Write two situations when you have demonstrated persistence.

Think about people you know (friends, family, classmates). Identify one person you know who has shown persistence.

Now describe a situation where this person has shown persistence. What actions showed they were persistent?

Student Tip #8

Explore assistive technology, especially if you've never tried it before.

Assistive technology (AT) is any item, piece of equipment, or software program that is used to increase, maintain, or improve the capabilities of an individual with a disability. In college, AT is usually referred to as technology that helps a student access their academic course content and assignments. AT can be no-tech, low-tech, or high-tech. Some examples of AT include:

- A computer program that helps with spelling.
- Enlarged font or worksheets for students with visual impairments.
- An app that reads electronic textbooks aloud for students with learning differences such as dyslexia.

AT tools are not expensive – some are even free. AT tools are available to all students who want to purchase them, but a few AT tools are available for free to students with a diagnosed disability. Your campus Accessibility Office will be knowledgeable about the forms of AT that are available to you. AT makes accessing academic content easier, but you may need to spend some time with it on your device to train it and become familiar with it. If you have never used AT, you should definitely explore it. Ask your Accessibility Office about AT and if there is an AT specialist on campus you can contact.

To Do

1. Go to your college website.

2. Find the Accessibility Office, Student Success Center, or Tutoring Center on the website.

3. Search for academic tools, apps, or technologies that are suggested to students.

List below the academic tools, apps, or technologies the college recommends on their website.

Student Tip #9

Ask for help.

Asking for help may sound like a simple thing to do, but some students find it very difficult. Asking for help requires you to do two things: 1) acknowledge that you need help, and 2) have the courage to ask for it. How do you know if you need help? In high school, you may have had a teacher or staff member who offered to help before you even asked. Or maybe your parents helped you at home. In college, there are many resources to help you, but YOU have to realize when you need help, and YOU need to ask for it.

College professors have office hours if you would like to meet with them to ask questions, and tutors are available to help you with specific class topics. The big difference between high school and college is that help options were typically built into your day during high school (whether you needed help or not), but in college you must seek them out. College students need to recognize when they need help, and then seek out the staff members or campus departments that can help. College professors list on their class syllabus the days and times they will be available to meet with students. These are called "office hours." Do not assume your professor will be in their office and available to talk to you if you show up unannounced outside of their office hours. When asking for help, you may need to email the professor or staff member first to arrange a meeting day/time. One of the most important pieces of advice I can give you is this – don't be afraid to ask for help. Successful students are not always the smartest students; they are often the students who ask for help when they need it. This will be you!

Think About It

Research has shown that college students who ask for help when they struggle are more successful than students who don't ask for help. Why do you think students might not ask for help?

List 3 reasons why students might be reluctant to ask for help.

Now write 3 positive outcomes that could happen if students ask for help in college.

Student Tip #10

Know the names and contact information of your Resident Assistants.

Resident Assistants (RAs) are the big brothers and big sisters of college residence halls. They are upper class students who often go through a rigorous interview process before they are selected to be RAs. They are student leaders who want to have responsibilities and leadership roles in the residence halls. They will have a dorm room on your floor or in your residence hall, and are your go to person if you have questions or needs. RAs want to help you. Maybe you will want to be an RA someday, too!

RAs should be your first stop if you have a question about anything, including which professors are good instructors, which clubs are active on campus, what to do if you lose your dorm room key/fob, where to find local restaurants/coffee shops/hair salons, etc. RAs are the face-to-face version of a Google Assistant®, so get to know them!

To Do

1. Go to your college website.

2. Search for the Residence Life or Living on Campus section of the website.

3. Research the different types of housing options and residence life support that are present on and off campus.

List the different types of people that work in the Residence Life office and in the residence halls.

"A river cuts through rock, not because of its power, but because of its persistence."

-James N. Watkins

"The secret of getting ahead is getting started."

-Mark Twain

Student Tip #11

Find the best place for you to do homework.

Where do you do homework now – in your bedroom, at a desk, at the dining room table? Why did you chose this place? Is this area quiet? Are you most productive when you sit in a chair at a desk? Do you prefer being comfortable and sitting on your bed? It's important to think about why you chose this location, because at college you will want to find a similar location to do your homework.

If you are most productive doing homework in your bedroom, your college dorm room might be the ideal environment for you. If you like working in a quiet space, then the campus library might be the perfect spot. If you prefer comfortable seating, then sitting on a couch in the campus student center or a nearby coffee shop might be just right.

Most college campuses have many different types of spaces for students to work, hang out, and socialize. Spend some time thinking about your current study and homework habits, and then think about the ideal college environment for you to study and learn. You can even try a few different spots on campus to find one that makes you feel the most comfortable and productive. Remember, learning is the main reason you are attending college!

Think About It

When you go to college you will want to find a place to do homework that allows you to be comfortable AND successful. Think about how you do your homework right now as you answer the questions below.

Where do you sit - At a desk? On your bed? At a table?

What type of sounds are nearby – Do you need complete silence (library), some noise, white noise or music (coffee shop)?

What temperature do you need to be productive – Do you like a fan, use a blanket, do you like being warm or cold?

What do you see – Do you face a wall, a window, etc.?

Based on your answers, identify 1 place on campus where you could do homework.

Student Tip #12

Pick one day every week to do your laundry. (Clothes AND bedding!)

A less talked about (but very important) part of college is personal cleanliness. The way you look and smell can affect your ability to make friends, and develop personal and professional relationships. I'm sure you prefer to be around someone whose breath smells good, hair is brushed, and clothes are clean. Likewise, other college students and professors want (and expect) the same from you. Therefore, it's important for you to make sure your hair looks good, your clothes look clean, and your breath smells good at all times.

One way for you to make sure you are always presentable is to shower every day and clean your clothes, towels, bed sheets, and pillow cases regularly. I recommend that you choose one day each week, the same day, to do your laundry. Remember, your clothes, towels, bed sheets, AND pillow cases need to be clean if you are to be clean.

Sometimes students remember to shower and use perfume or deodorant, but they forget to do their laundry. Choose a day for laundry when you don't have a lot going on; most students choose Saturday or Sunday. Laundry rooms can be really busy on the weekends, so it's best to choose a time when most other students are not likely to be doing laundry. The least busy times in the laundry room are usually early in the morning (before 10:00 a.m.) and late at night (10:00 p.m. or later).

Real Life Scenario

Alycia is a student-athlete who plays basketball and has practices or games every night that start around 6:00 p.m. and last until 9:00 p.m. She has classes on Monday, Wednesday and Friday that begin at 10:30 a.m. and last until 5:00 p.m. when she eats dinner before practice. Her classes on Tuesday and Thursday start at 1:10 p.m. and last until 5:45p.m. On the weekends Alycia does not have basketball practice but she likes to sleep in and then go to lunch at 12:00 noon. Alycia follows her team rules about not partying at night, so she usually stays in her dorm room with friends and hangs out on the weekends.

Alycia is having trouble finding a time to do her laundry each week because she is busy with basketball practice and classes.

Thinking about Alycia's schedule, what are some times that Alycia could do laundry on Monday, Wednesday and Friday?

What are some times that Alycia could do laundry on Tuesday and Thursday?

What are some times that Alycia could do laundry on Saturday and Sunday?

If you were Alycia, when would YOU choose to do your laundry?

Student Tip #13

Respect your roommate's space by keeping your belongings on your side of the dorm room.

Imagine you own a car and a friend asks to borrow the car to go to the mall. The friend returns from the mall and thanks you for letting them borrow the car. The next day you get in the car and notice there are empty soda bottles, gum wrappers, and candy bar wrappers on the floor and seat. You realize your friend borrowed your car and left their garbage inside! Your friend did not respect your space or belongings. Respecting someone else's space is important in your college dorm room, too.

If you decide to live on campus, you will probably have a roommate. Basically, you will be sharing a small dorm room with a stranger. Think about your dorm room as having two halves: one-half is yours and one-half is theirs. All of your belongings need to stay on your half of the room. This includes your bed, dresser, garbage can, clothes, shoes, backpack, toiletries, etc. If you leave your clothes (clean or dirty) on your roommate's side of the room, it's like you left empty soda bottles in their car.

It's important to respect your roommate's space, and accept that half of the room is theirs. Keep your belongings on your side of the room. If you and your roommate have a conversation and agree to share space, that's great! But don't assume that leaving your shoes, clothes and garbage on their side of the room is okay.

Stay on your side of the room, unless you are invited into your roommate's space. If you respect your roommate's space, they are more likely to respect yours.

Real Life Scenario

Natalia is a college freshman who lives on campus with her roommate, Madison. On the weekends, Madison goes home so Natalia has the room to herself. Natalia invites a few friends over on the weekends to hang out and listen to music in her dorm room. They usually order pizza and have snacks. One Sunday night, Madison returns to campus and when she enters the dorm room she notices there are food crumbs and chip bag wrappers on her bed. Madison gets upset and asks Natalia why there are crumbs and food wrappers on her bed. Natalia said that she had a few friends over this weekend and it was no big deal.

Why do you think Madison is upset?

What are some topics that Natalia and Madison should talk about in regards to sharing space?

Student Tip #14

Even if you put in a lot of effort, college still might be hard.

This tip is one of the hardest tips in this book for students to understand. You may have received good grades in high school based, in part, on your effort. For example, imagine that one of your high school teachers asked you to write a two-page paper about climate change. You work really hard for about 10 hours studying the subject, brainstorming, organizing your thoughts, outlining your approach, and then writing and editing your paper. However, although you worked very hard, you could only write one page. When you turn in your paper, your high school teacher says, "Even though your paper is only one page, I can tell you worked very hard. Your paper has good ideas, so you earned a B."

In college, things might be different. When you turn in your one-page paper, your college professor says "I can tell you worked very hard, and your paper has good ideas. But your paper is not the required two pages, so you earned an F."

What!? Why do these scenarios end so differently? It's because college professors grade you on the work you produce, not your effort. Professors don't care how long you worked on an assignment. They only care about the finished product. This is a big difference between high school and college. This is why college can be hard.

If college is hard for you, keep at it. Be persistent (more in Student Tip #7). If you are struggling in college, reach out for help (more in Student Tip #9). The more you follow the advice in Student Tips #7 and #9, the easier college will become. Don't give up when things get hard. You can do it!

Think About It

Think about difficult situations you have dealt with in high school. Write down 2 situations that were hard for you (in school or outside of school) and how you dealt with those tough situations.

These situations were good practice for challenging situations you may have in college (and in life). Remember, don't give up when you face difficult situations. Keep going!

Student Tip #15

Find out where the health center and counseling centers are located – even if you don't need them now.

Every college and university has a health center which provides medical care and also a counseling center for students who need mental health supports. Even if you don't need to talk with a therapist right now or haven't talked with one in the past, a situation may arise sometime in your college career when you may want to talk with a counselor. Another reason to know the location of your campus counseling center is to be a support for others on campus (perhaps a friend or roommate) who may need counseling services. Find out the location (building on campus), hours of operation, name of counselors who work there, and if there is an emergency line for needs outside of operating hours. If you are a student who currently uses a counselor, it is a good idea to make a connection with your campus health center before you begin college if you want to use their supports instead of a counselor from home. Your mental and emotional health is just as important as your academic success. Even if you think you won't need these supports it is still a good idea to know that they are there in case you do.

To Do

1. Go to your college website.

2. Find the Student Life or Campus Life section of the website.

3. Search for the various Health & Wellness services that are offered on campus. Search for physical health services (walk-in clinic, nurse/doctor on staff) and mental health supports (counseling center, peer support groups, 24 hr helplines).

List below the physical health services listed on the website:

After doing your search, do you have any remaining questions about physical health services on campus?

List below the mental health services listed on the website:

After doing your search, do you have any remaining questions about mental health services on campus?

Student Tip #16

Keep a consistent sleep schedule.

I believe this is one of the MOST important tips in this book. A consistent sleep schedule can greatly enhance your college experience by keeping your mind and body functioning in a healthy way. Sleep really does affect your ability to do your best work! Getting enough sleep provides you with the best chance for success. For example, healthy sleep habits will help you waking up for class, arriving at class on time, remembering what you learn in class, and doing homework. Studies show that losing one night of sleep – perhaps by pulling an all-nighter – can adversely affect your physical and mental health for the next seven days.

I have seen too many cases where a student stays up until 3:00 a.m., sleeps all day until 3:00 p.m., eats dinner, and is wide awake until 3:00 a.m. again. When a student's sleep schedule is reversed (asleep during the day, and awake at night), it can be very hard (and take a long time) to flip your sleep schedule back to normal. Research shows that adults who work during the third shift (overnight) are less alert, less coordinated, and less productive at their jobs. Our bodies aren't meant to be awake at night. The bottom line is: playing video games or socializing until 2:00 a.m. is not as important as getting a good night's sleep!

Think About It

Think about your current sleep schedule. How many hours do you usually sleep during the weekdays? On the weekends?

What kind of environment do you need in order for you to fall asleep? Think about lights on/lights off, noise/no noise, temperature of the room, lots of blankets/no blankets, etc. Write your ideal sleeping environment below:

What is one challenge that you have now to getting enough sleep (staying up late watching videos, playing video games, texting, etc.)? Identify 1 way that you will try to overcome this barrier in college.

Student Tip #17

Keep important personal items (medicine, money, etc.) in a drawer or out of sight.

Having a roommate in college means that students you don't know (friends of your roommate) may enter your personal space. It's important to have a secure place in your room to keep your important personal belongings (such as medications, money, etc.). I hope that everyone you meet in college will be honest and trustworthy, but that might not be the case.

Suppose you were walking across campus and saw a wallet on the ground with a student ID, credit card, and cash inside. What would you do? Some students would bring the wallet to the Campus Safety office, where the "lost and found" is located. Other students might decide to keep the wallet, and try to use the credit card (which doesn't belong to them), and spend the money (which also doesn't belong to them).

Now imagine the lost wallet was yours. What would you want the student who found your wallet to do with it? I bet you would want them to bring your wallet to the Campus Safety office without spending your money, right? This example might seem a little silly, but it illustrates the types of moral choices you and other students will have to make in college.

Now let's apply this example to your dorm room. If you leave your purse, wallet, or medication bottles on your desk, and your roommate invites friends over, it becomes similar to the lost wallet scenario. You hope your roommate's friends will leave your personal belongings alone, but not all students are honest and trustworthy. How can you prevent strangers from taking your important personal items?

Colleges recommend that students buy a lock box for their dorm room. A lock box is a metal box that requires a key or code to open it. It's a perfect place to keep medication bottles, usernames / passwords, important papers, credit cards, wallets, etc. It may be small enough to fit in a desk drawer, or large enough to fit under your bed. Another alternative is to purchase a locking 2 drawer file cabinet. A file cabinet can be locked and also provide storage space for other items. Both items are fairly inexpensive and are good investments.

Think About It

Identify some important belongings that you have at home and write them below. (Examples: wallet, phone, medication, jewelry, money, credit cards, important papers, etc.)

Where do you keep these important belongings at home? Do you keep them in your bedroom? Does a parent hold onto them? Do you have a special drawer/file cabinet? In your backpack?

Brainstorm 2 places that you could put these important belongings when you go to college.

Student Tip #18

Write down usernames and passwords for your college email address, portal log-in, etc.

Each college and university is different, but all schools will assign new college students an email address. Also, most colleges will require you to set up an account in an online learning management system, similar to PowerSchool®, where you can check your grades and course schedule, request a copy of your transcripts, etc. Also, some professors will require that you submit assignments online using the college's learning management system. (Some professors might prefer that you personally turn in a paper copy of your assignments.)

As you can see, you will be required to create multiple new accounts, which require usernames and passwords. Remembering all of your college usernames and password can be tough. It's a good idea to find an organizational system that you like and that works for you BEFORE you arrive on campus.

There are great apps for your phone that store and organize usernames and passwords. You can even send important account log-in information to your parents as a backup, in case you lose your phone or your primary method fails.

Think About It

What are the different accounts that you have right now that you need to remember usernames & passwords? Write the accounts (do not write the usernames /passwords) below:

What is the method that you use right now to remember your usernames/passwords? Do you write them in a book, use an app, save them in your email/smartphone? If you have trouble remembering this information that is okay too. Write HOW you store this information below:

You will be required to use new accounts and emil addresses that are given to you by your college. What is one method that you could use next year to store or remember your usernames and passwords?

Student Tip #19

Personal hygiene – keep it private.

Getting privacy in a college dorm room can be tricky. Sharing a room requires that all roommates understand and respect each other's personal boundaries (more in Student Tip #4). For example, you may not feel comfortable changing clothes in front of your roommate, but your roommate may feel completely comfortable changing in front of you! Talk to your roommate at the beginning of the semester about privacy and personal boundaries, even if the conversation is uncomfortable or awkward.

Also, you should have a conversation with your roommate about having overnight guests in the dorm room. Are you both comfortable with this? Do you need to ask each other's permission first? Are guests allowed to leave belongings in the room? At most colleges and universities if you are living on campus your RA will encourage or require that roommates complete a roommate agreement form. This is an excellent opportunity to talk about some of those potentially akward things without having to bring them up once there is an issue.

Remember, to have true privacy, your dorm room door AND blinds must be closed. I have heard students say "I don't need to close my blinds because I'm on the top floor." Whether it is day or night, if your dorm room light is on and your blinds are open, students can see you. So close your blinds/shades when you change – every time!

Think About It

Think about personal hygiene routines that you have now and where you do those routines. Where do you shave, change clothes, brush your teeth, brush your hair, take medication, etc.? Maybe you have a medical condition that requires you to do other medical tasks (such as changing a bandage, using a medical device, etc.). If you do these personal hygiene tasks now in private, you should consider where you will do these tasks in college if you live with a roommate and share a common bathroom with other students on your residence hall.

List any thoughts or questions below on the topic of privacy in your residence hall.

Student Tip #20

Know when to contact your RA, Campus Safety, or call 911.

No one wants to imagine that emergencies will happen at college, but occasionally a situation will occur when you need to ask for help. When you arrive on campus be sure to know the location or building of the Campus Safety office, Residence Life office, Student Union, etc. It's important to know WHEN to ask for help and WHO to contact for different levels of help. For example, you might need to ask for help if you lose your dorm room key or get locked out of your dorm room. You also might need help if there is a leak in your dorm room window or ceiling. You might need help if you are walking on campus and twist your ankle or if a friend with epilepsy has a seizure in their dorm room.

Some students might find it helpful to make a list of IF... THEN... scenarios and hang up this list on their dorm room wall to help them remember WHEN and WHO to ask for help. Remember, in college your parents will not be with you, so you will be more independent in your academic and social life, as well as situations in which conflicts arise. You may have experience resolving conflicts in your high school or at home, but it may take some time to adjust to the support systems at your college, and knowing when and who to ask for help if you need it.

Real Life Scenario

Read the scenarios below and identify if the situation would require you to contact your dorm Resident Assistant, Campus Safety or call 911.

You are attending an Anime Student Club meeting on campus and the meeting ends at 11pm. You feel nervous walking back to your dorm in the dark. Who should you contact?

You can't get to sleep at night because the room next door is playing loud music. You have asked them to turn the music down and they said that it is the weekend and they are allowed to have fun. Who do you contact?

You are hanging out in your friend's dorm room when he starts to have a seizure. You aren't sure what to do because your friend has never had a seizure before. Who should you contact?

You park your car in a student parking lot and walk to class. When you return to your car it looks like another car hit your car and your taillight is broken and bumper is scratched. Who could you contact?

"If you don't like something, change it. If you can't change it, change your attitude."

-Maya Angelou

"All things are difficult before they are easy."

-Thomas Fuller

Student Tip #21

Visit each professor at least once per semester in their office.

During my freshman year in college, a friend gave me this advice and I have remembered it ever since- "At least once per semester, visit your professors in their office." This advice is as relevant today as it was when I was in college. You might have a question about an assignment or an upcoming exam or you might not need anything at all, but making the effort to visit your professors will help them get to know the amazing person that you are!

You have probably heard the saying: "Students at large universities are only known as a number." This saying means that if your professors don't get to know you personally, then they will only know you by your student ID number. In college, you WANT professors to know you by name, know your learning style, and know how they can help you be successful.

Unlike high school, YOU need to make the first move in college. YOU need to schedule appointments with your professors; they will not schedule appointments with you. So go ahead and schedule a meeting with your professors at least once per semester, even if you don't need any help. During this meeting you can introduce yourself to the professor, talk about your major, what you are enjoying about their class, etc. Trust me, it will help you develop a relationship with them that can help you now and also down the road.

Think About It

Think about your high school teachers this year and previous years. You probably liked the teaching style of some teachers more than others. For example, some teachers like to tell stories while others follow an agenda or lesson plan the same way every class. Think about some of your favorite high school teachers. Why did you like them? What was their teaching style? Write your thoughts about WHY you liked some of your high school teachers below.

Student Tip #22

Put yourself in social situations – even if it's uncomfortable.

College offers brand new academic and social opportunities. College classes and coursework are important, but college is also about making new friends and exploring social events and activities. Your college friends will be there to have fun with you when you need a break from your studies and homework; they will also be your support system while you are away from home. For students with social anxiety or shyness, the transition to an unstructured social environment can be challenging. Most first-year college students feel some degree of nervousness and excitement at the thought of meeting new people. Push yourself to work through any social nervousness you may have.

Saying hello is a great way to break the ice and initiate a conversation. Say hello to the workers in the dining hall. Say hello to your RAs when you see them in your dorm. Take advantage of every new opportunity and chance meeting, especially during your first few weeks on campus.

Attend student club meetings – even if you're not sure you're interested. Attend club fairs to find out what activities and extracurricular clubs are offered on campus. Attend speeches by guest speakers, and evening activities held in the University Union and residence halls. Know that most first year students feel the same nervousness and excitement that you do at the thought of meeting new people. You are not alone.

Real Life Scenario

Monique is a college freshman who spends many hours each night in her dorm room doing homework. She is feeling homesick and stays in her room calling her parents and friends from home. She is nervous about meeting new people and hasn't made new friends yet at college. One evening her Resident Assistant knocks on her door to say hello. The RA lets Monique know that all of the rooms on the floor of her residence hall are having an ice cream social later that night. At the event, first year students who live in Monique's residence hall will make ice cream sundaes and get to know each other. The RA asks Monique if she wants to attend.

What could be a possible outcome if Monique does <u>not</u> attend the ice cream social?

What could be a possible outcome if Monique <u>does</u> attend the ice cream social?

What would YOU do in this situation if you were Monique? Why?

Student Tip #23

Know your learning style.

We all have qualities that make us unique; some of our traits are strengths and some are weaknesses. For example, one of my traits is that I struggle at drawing – I'm terrible! Another one of my traits is that I am not very productive at night, and usually fall asleep early. On the other hand, I can be annoyingly productive in the early morning. Knowing these two qualities about myself helped me choose my college classes. I stayed away from drawing and art classes. (I probably could have worked really hard in an art class, and might have passed the class, but it didn't play to my strengths.) Likewise, I chose not to take a three-hour evening class that met once per week because I probably would have fallen asleep. (Again, it didn't play to my strengths.) I knew I was a morning person, so I signed up for college classes that were held in the morning. It's important to know your learning style because you will be able to choose the classes that play to your strengths.

Besides choosing your classes, you will get to make many other decisions in college. For example, the location of your dorm room, the number of roommates you will have, the time of day you exercise and when you decide to eat meals in the dining hall, etc. If you have never thought about these choices before, start now! The college staff expect you to speak up for what you want. Speaking up for yourself and the way you learn is called self-advocacy (more in Student Tip #24).

Think About It

There are three types of learning styles; visual, auditory and kinesthetic. Everyone is a mixture of these learning styles but we each tend to learn best in primarily one of these methods. Think about your high school classes and teachers. Do you enjoy learning from teachers who lecture and tell stories? If you enjoy learning by listening, then you may be an auditory learner.

Do you enjoy teachers who use videos, PowerPoint presentations, and write notes and diagrams on the board? If so, you may be a visual learner.

Do you enjoy learning in classes that allow you to participate in hands-on activities in class? If this describes how you learn best, you may be a kinesthetic learner.

Which of these learning styles describes how you learn best? Can you provide an example?

Student Tip #24

Speaking up for yourself is important.

In college, if you don't say anything about a problem, the college staff and professors will assume that you have everything under control. If you are having trouble with anything (classes, roommate, mental health, etc.), YOU need to speak up.

This tip applies to both high school and college students, but especially college students. In college, no one will know your likes, dislikes, learning style, or how your teachers helped you learn in high school. YOU need to talk about these topics – your parents can't talk to the college academic staff like they could when you were in high school. If you have a question about a homework assignment, YOU need to talk to the professor after class, or send them an email with your question. If you need a tutoring appointment, YOU need to find the tutoring center on campus and make an appointment in person or online. If you lose your dorm room key, YOU need to notify the Campus Safety office or your RA.

Think About It

Who usually speaks up for you now when you need help or have a question in school – is it you? Is it your parents? Who usually speaks up for you when you need help or have a question about extracurricular activities outside of school (sports team, band or chorus, drama club, your job, volunteer opportunity, etc.)?

Write 1 scenario that happened recently when you needed to ask for help or had a question. Next, write WHO asked for help or spoke up in that scenario.

If YOU were the person who asked for help in the scenario above, write 1 positive skill that you used when you asked for help. If someone else spoke up for you (such as a parent), write 1 way that you can begin to work on the skill of speaking up for yourself in college.

Student Tip #25

Remember to keep your devices charged.

Will a videogame system work without power? No. Will a microwave work if it's not plugged in? No. Without electricity, all of your electrical appliances are useless. Likewise, if you forget to charge your battery-powered devices, they won't be available when you need them to take notes in class, type homework assignments, or maybe even read a textbook online. It's VERY important to remember to charge the battery-powered devices you will need the following day (such as your phone, laptop computer, and/or tablet).

In Student Tip #6, I recommended bringing multiple power charging cords to college. Put a charging cord next to your bed, and another on your desk in your dorm room. Charge your important devices EVERY night. Creating a charging routine at bedtime will help you develop a habit to keep your devices charged and ready to go!

Think About It

Think about the devices you use in high school both at home and at school that need to be charged to keep their power. Write any devices that you use below:

How do you remember to charge these devices? Do you plug them in at a certain time of day? Where are they plugged in at home or at school?

How many charging cords do you require for all of these devices? In college you will need the number of charging cords that you use now (plus 1 or 2 more – the Power of Multiples!). Write down the number of charging and power extension cords you will need to bring to college.

Student Tip #26

Understand how your disability affects you.

Knowing what your disability is, and understanding how it affects you, are two different things. For example, I know that rockets leave the earth and fly into space. But do I understand how a rocket works? Absolutely not! Likewise, you may know that you have been diagnosed with dyslexia, for example, but you may not understand how it will affect you in college.

The best way to understand your disability is to ask. Ask your parents, your high school teachers, your guidance counselor or coach. These people can help you think about the ways your disability may affect you in college. Because you have (probably) never been to college before, it might be hard for you, alone, to imagine how your disability will affect you there.

Understanding your disability can help you self-advocate (there's that word again!), and ask for tools to help you be successful.

Think About It

Knowing how your disability affects you in high school can help you prepare for college. You will be ahead of the game if you have already thought about the questions below.

How could your disability or medical condition affect you residentially at college?

How could your disability or medical condition affect you academically at college?

How could your disability or medical condition affect you socially (making friendships, getting along with your roommate, at social events) at college?

Student Tip #27

If you need accommodations, ask for them.

College is a brand new environment where every first-year student starts over with a clean slate. You know nothing about the other students and professors, and they know nothing about you. This means that no one will know if you have a learning disability, medical condition, or mental health challenge unless you tell them. Therefore, it's up to YOU to ask for the tools that will help you be successful in class, on campus, etc. Tools that you need to be successful as a result of your disability are called accommodations.

For example, if you have difficulty taking notes while listening to a teacher speak because of a learning or physical disability, an accommodation may be receiving a copy of the teacher's notes, or using note taking and/or recording software. Other possible accommodations are extended time on tests and taking exams in a distraction-reduced environment.

All colleges provide accommodations to eligible students, but YOU must apply for them. Your parents cannot do it for you. If you need an accommodation, it's up to YOU to make an appointment with the Accessibility Office, bring documentation of your disability to the appointment, and explain why and how an accommodation will help you.

Ultimately, it's your choice whether or not to disclose your disability to the college staff, but, as you can see, there could be significant benefits to doing so. Spend some time thinking about what is the right choice for you – to disclose or not to disclose your disability.

Think About It

In high school, accommodations are typically built into students' schedules so students don't need to ask for them. Ideally, students have been involved in the IEP / 504 process in high school so they know the accommodations they are receiving. This is a great time to start thinking about the types of support you may have already and the support that you will need in college. Let's get started - Think about your high school experience by answering these questions:

Did you receive academic accommodations in high school?
If you answered yes, write the accommodations you received in the space below.

If you answered no, can you think of any accommodations that may be helpful in your future college classes or college experience?

If you answered 'I'm not sure', this is a good opportunity to talk with your family or teachers. They can share with you whether or not you are receiving accommodations in high school and, if you are, they can identify the types of support you have in place.

Student Tip #28

Visit the campus Accessibility Office – it's a great resource!

By law, every college and university is required to provide reasonable accommodations for students with diagnosed disabilities. The staff in the Accessibility Office are there to provide you with accommodations to help you access your class content. This office is not a tutoring center – they will not help you with your homework. But they will…

- Talk with you about how your disability affects you in the classroom, in residence halls, etc.
- Review documents that you have which verifies your disability.
- Help you solve conflicts you might be having with your professors because of your disability.
- Talk with you about assistive technology that could help you in the classroom (such as programs to help you take notes, organize your thoughts, and assist with spelling). For more about Assistive Technology, see Student Tip #8.

The Accessibility Office is a very important resource for students with disabilities. The office staff are smart, experienced, and friendly. Get to know them! I recommend visiting this office two or three times each semester. The more often you visit and share about yourself, the better able the staff will be to help you throughout your college career.

To Do

1. Go to your college website.

2. Find the Accessibility Office, Disability Services or Academic Support section of the website.

Identify the building and room location of this office.

Identify the hours of operation of this office.

List the names of the staff members who work in this office.

List the ways that you can contact the Accessibility Office (email address, phone number, social media channels, etc.).

Student Tip #29

Be independent, but don't be too proud to ask for help.

Many students who receive special education services in high school (such as working with a special education teacher, visiting a resource room, talking to a counselor or school psychologist, etc.) want to be independent in college. I applaud you! Being independent is important; it's a goal that colleges want you to achieve by the time you graduate. However, sometimes students are so determined to "do college on their own" that they refuse to ask for help.

Some students think that asking for help makes them appear weak. But that isn't the case at all! If the New York Yankees or Boston Red Sox brought in a new pitching coach to help their pitchers, would you think their pitchers were weak? Of course not! It simply means the Yankees (or the Red Sox) want their pitchers to perform at their best! This is why you should ask for help in college – so that you can perform at your best, too.

If you are struggling, ask for help. Being independent is a great quality, but if you start to struggle, reach out for help. If you're struggling in an area that is affected by your disability, visit the Accessibility Office (see Student Tip #28). Your Academic Advisor is another person on campus that is a great resource to seek out when you need help. They can guide you on resolving academic issues and connect you with other staff members on campus who can help if you are struggling in other areas. Definitely get to know your Academic Advisor!

Real Life Scenario

Emma is a college freshman who struggled with depression throughout high school. She met with a counselor once a week in high school and decided to stop seeing a counselor in college because she feels like she is ready to try college on her own. Emma has a successful first 2 weeks of college! In mid-September she starts to feel overwhelmed by her coursework and has some small arguments with her roommate. Emma notices that she is spending more time alone in her room and has trouble sleeping. When her parents call, Emma doesn't want to disappoint them so she tells them that everything is fine. By the end of September Emma is completely overwhelmed, oversleeping and missing classes, and not eating 3 meals a day. Emma thinks the campus counselor won't understand what she is going through and so she doesn't want to ask for help.

What advice would you give to Emma?

Who are some of the people that Emma could go to for help (emotional or academic)?

Student Tip #30

Don't guess how well you're doing in your classes – find out!

The college year is made up of two semesters – fall (September through December) and spring (January through May). Each semester lasts about 15 weeks. A college semester is like a novel because it has a beginning, middle, and end. At the beginning of the semester, the professors will introduce the class and themselves to you; toward the middle of the semester, you may be given small projects and midterm exams (which might test you on everything you learned in the first half of the semester); and toward the end of the semester, you will usually be given big projects and final exams.

All of this is important to understand because a semester can pass quickly. At any point in the semester, you should know the grade you are earning. If you don't know your grade, find out. Colleges provide midterm grades and final grades, and sometimes an early academic report three to four weeks into the semester. But if you wait until the college provides you with a report, it may be too late to improve your grades by the end of the semester.

College professors do not keep their students informed of their class grades. It's up to YOU to find out. The easiest way to find out your grades at any time in the semester is to look on your college's online management system or portal. Or you can look at the grades on papers that your professors give back to you. Knowing your grades will also make conversations with your parents easier. When you start college, your parents' favorite question will be "How are your classes going?" (Trust me.)

Real Life Scenario

Michael is an avid gamer who enjoys playing video games at home and online with friends. At the beginning of college, Michael meets many new friends who enjoy playing video games too! Michael and his friends play video games until 2:00 a.m. or 3:00 a.m. every night and, although he is tired, Michael attends every class. However, Michael doesn't spend any time doing homework. In high school, Michael's teachers would remind him to turn in missing assignments. In college, none of his professors have approached him about his missing homework so Michael assumes he is doing well in his courses. When midterm grades are entered by professors in October, Michael is shocked to see 4 F's! Michael didn't realize he was failing his classes and is upset that no one told him.

Why do you think Michael is failing his classes?

Identify 2 ways that Michael could have discovered how he was doing in each class during the semester.

What suggestion would you give to help Michael get back on track in his classes?

Words of Advice for Families

Family Tip #1

College is a marathon, not a sprint.

Change takes time. Developing your student's high school skills into college-level academic, social, emotional, and executive functioning skills takes time. Once you accept this, your student's college journey will become much easier – for YOU. The path to your student's success won't be a straight line. They will experience progress and setbacks, forward steps and side steps. Progress will seem to be stalled, and then they will make amazing gains. Some classes will be challenging, while others will play to their strengths. It's all part of the journey.

Whatever direction they travel, they were meant to travel on that path. Walk alongside them. The person that enters college will not be the same person that graduates. Trust the process and settle in for the marathon.

Think About It

Anything that is worthwhile takes time to accomplish. Look at the images below. Which image do you HOPE your student's college journey will look like? Which image do you think will ACTUALLY look like your student's college journey?

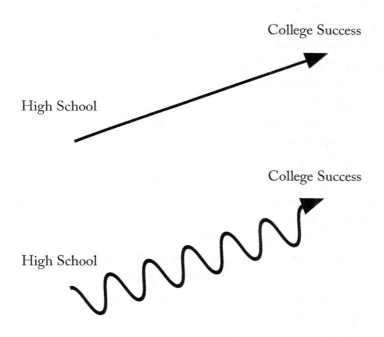

Family Tip #2

Improve your student's executive functioning skills NOW.

Executive functioning, or EF, skills play a crucial role in college success – probably a more important role than most parents realize. EF skills are responsible for coordinating your student's time management, organization, self-regulation, planning, and prioritization skills. EF skills have been compared to the conductor of an orchestra – coordinating the other skills in the brain to function smoothly and efficiently with each other. Typically, EF skills don't fully develop in the human brain until the age of 25. This means that your college student will be tasked to use EF skills that are not fully developed!

Your student's EF skills will impact ALL aspects of their college experience, including academic, social, and residential success. In high school, your student's EF skills may have been supported by teachers, guidance counselors, school psychologists, parents, and strategies that you placed in the home environment (such as calendars, waking your student in the morning, and giving reminders to complete their homework). In college, these external supports will disappear. Your student will be expected to have internalized these EF skills and are solely responsible to manage their own EF skills and strategies.

If your student currently struggles with any of the EF skills mentioned above, they will probably struggle in college in these same areas – unless you start developing these skills now. Start working on these skills BEFORE your student goes to college. The good news is through repetition EF skills can be improved!

Here are some specific examples of how you can help your student improve EF skills:

Manage their own schedule: Help your student independently manage their daily and weekly schedules through the use of a visual calendar they update every day, or by using an app like Google Calendar®. Paper calendars can be created on the computer, printed, and hung on a wall. There are also whiteboard calendars that come in weekly or monthly varieties; some which can be hung on a wall, the back of a bedroom door, or even magnetic calendars that can stick to a refrigerator door.

Wake up to an alarm in the morning: This is one of the most important tips for new college students (more in Student Tip #2). While in high school, have your student practice setting an alarm on their smartphone or using an alarm clock to wake up. Better yet, use both of these methods. If your student doesn't wake up easily, explore other types of alarms. There are alarms that vibrate under your student's pillow, alarm clocks on wheels that will roll across the floor when going off to force your student to get out of bed to turn it off, and smartphone apps that require your student to solve math problems before turning off the alarm!

Manage their own hygiene routine: Does your student need reminders to shower or take medication? Your student can practice setting alarm reminders using the "Clock" function on their smartphone. Also, consider providing your student with a voice-activated smart device in their bedroom. Some students even bring this device with them to college! Your student can tell the device to set reminders for their personal hygiene routine.

"Happiness is not found in things you possess, but in what you have the courage to release."

-Nathaniel Hawthorne

"Only when he no longer knows what he is doing does the painter do good things."

-Edgar Degas

Family Tip #3

Only buy dorm room "essentials" that your student will use.

In my experience, families enjoy back-to-school shopping because of the endless totes, crates, bins, organizers, hooks/hangers, dorm furniture, etc. that stores advertise in the summer as "dorm room essentials." Many families unpack their purchases for the first time in their student's dorm room. If your student didn't use a three-tiered organizer in their bedroom at home, how will they know how to use one in their dorm room?

Imagine that you are used to driving a car with an automatic transmission. Then you buy a car with a manual transmission. You would need to practice with the manual transmission before you felt comfortable. Similarly, your student won't be comfortable with new organizational tools unless they have had time to become familiar with them. If he or she did NOT use something at home, he or she most likely will NOT use it at college (even if it was on sale and called a Dorm Essential!). Spend time practicing with these tools at home before you bring them to college.

To clarify, I'm not suggesting that you open every back to school organizational tool / furniture box at home before bringing it to college. Boxes are much easier to fit into your car on move-in day! But I am suggesting that you think about the teenager you have at home now and shop for dorm room "essentials" with that person in mind.

Think About It

Think about the types of organizational tools that you use at home for your family. Do you have calendars that your family uses to write activities and events? Do you have calendars hung on a wall, a shared app on a phone, etc.? Do you use hooks to hang backpacks? Folders for papers from school?

What types of organizational tools do you use professionally or personally that help you to be productive?

What organizational tools does your student use? If you aren't sure, use this time to start a conversation with him/her. The tools he/she uses now will be the same tools he/she will use in college. If you discover that your student doesn't have many organizational tools and systems in place right now, this is a good time to start modeling the tools that work for you and encouraging your student to try new tools before he/she leaves for college (and before you spend money on dorm room essentials that will sit unused in boxes!).

Family Tip #4

Don't solve your student's problems until you ask THIS question first.

This is one of the hardest rules for parents of new college students to hear – so get ready. As parents, we have heard that doing everything for our children hinders their development. Instead we should guide our children and encourage them to develop new skills. When we allow our children to learn a new skill, or solve a problem themselves, we empower them. Even small successes will build confidence, and ultimately lead to independence.

Makes sense, right? Don't all parents want their children to be successful and independent problem solvers? Of course we do! However, the difficulty arises when parents can solve the problems quicker or do the tasks more easily than our children can. Solving a problem quickly for your student can be a very tempting option. Why would a parent let their four-year-old struggle to tie their shoes when they can tie the shoes for them? Why would a parent let their student struggle with a roommate conflict when they can call the roommate's mom and solve the problem? Because letting your student learn HOW to solve problems is much more valuable than doing it for them.

If your student calls and complains about a problem at college, it can be very tempting to tell them exactly what they should do, or personally make a call and quickly resolve the problem yourself. However, I challenge you to do this instead – BEFORE you offer advice, or jump in to solve the problem, ask your student, "How do YOU think YOU can solve this problem?"

You may get some resistance at first, especially if your student is accustomed to having you tell them exactly what to do, or step in on their behalf. But be firm; insist that they offer a solution. Your student may become frustrated and you may need to coax them toward the solution at first, but eventually, your student will learn to solve their own problems.

But learning comes after (and is on the other side) of frustration. So the next time you get a frantic text that reads, "I lost my room key. What should I do?" or, "I don't know how to do this homework assignment," or "My roommate is being too loud and I'm trying to sleep," try answering: "How do YOU think YOU can solve that problem?"

Think About It

Think about a recent problem or situation where your student asked you for help. How did you respond?

What was the outcome of the situation? What lessons do you think your student learned as a result of your response?

Family Tip #5

Your student will bring their high school academic and social skills to college – for better or worse.

When your child leaves high school he/she will have developed a set of skills (both academic and social) that were cultivated in high school and helped your child meet the demands of the high school environment. During the first few weeks or months of college, your student will rely heavily on the academic and social skills they utilized in high school. Some students may find that their high school skills are effective in college; these lucky students may not need to change or adjust their skill set. Other students may be surprised to learn that their high school skills are not successfully helping them meet the rigors of college. This is completely normal.

The most successful students are able to recognize which high school skills work, and which ones don't. Encourage your student to ask for help from the college staff when their high school skills aren't working. If your student is discouraged after the first few weeks or months of college, remind them that college is a marathon, and to be persistent (See Student Tip #7).

Think About It

When you drop off your student at college he/she will essentially be a new college freshman in the body of a high schooler. It takes time to get adjusted to college dorm life, college classes, more unstructured free time, etc. While your student is becoming acclimated to college life, expect him/her to act in similar ways as they did in high school.

Did she have a messy bedroom at home? Expect a messy dorm room in college.

Did he struggle with time management and playing too many video games in high school? Expect the same behavior in the first month or two of college.

Think about your student's areas of struggle and expect that he/she will have these same struggles in college – initially. The important take away is that their skills will improve and they will evolve into mature, independent college students....with time. But don't be surprised if you see the same high school student before your eyes in the fall semester.

Family Tip #6

Practice paying with a debit or credit card.

In college, there are many opportunities for students to use a debit or credit card. Your student might buy takeout food, buy snacks from a vending machine in their residence hall, go shopping with friends, order art supplies for class, pay for an Uber/Lyft ride, etc. Because there are so many opportunities for your student to make purchases, it's important that they know HOW to use a debit or credit card BEFORE they get to college.

To teach your student the value of money, I recommend taking your student to the grocery store with a grocery list and a grocery budget of, say, $100. Make sure your student pays close attention to the total cost as they accumulate the grocery items. Emphasize that there is a choice to make for each grocery item, and there is a difference between the best value and the cheapest cost.

I also recommend having your student make online purchases, purchase something at a retail store, and pay the bill at a restaurant using a debit or credit card. Speaking of restaurants, make sure your student can calculate the tip based on the total bill. You don't want your student's first experience paying a restaurant bill to be when they take their friend out for a birthday dinner, and leave a $100 tip because they have never paid a restaurant bill before.

Make sure your student is comfortable using their debit or credit card for any purchase you can think of. Most importantly, make sure your student can check the balance on their card, and understands the consequences of exceeding the card limit.

I also suggest setting a budget with your child for expenses outside of textbooks. Start small! You can always add more money to their account but you can't go back once all of the money is spent. Incidental charges and eating outside of the cafeteria can really add up! You should also consider having access to your child's banking account in order to see patterns in their spending habits. This is a personal decision and depends on your relationship with your child as well as their money management skills.

Think About It

Can your son/daughter use a grocery list and go into the grocery store to find the correct items?

Does your student know how to pay a bill at a restaurant, sign the check and then leave a tip?

If you're not sure, this is a great time to teach your student the skills of how to use a debit card / credit card at home.

Family Tip #7

Talk to your student about expectation for staying in touch with you.

As in life, many conflicts in college can be avoided by managing our expectations. For example, suppose you were hired for a new job with the expectation of being paid $1,000 every paycheck, but your first paycheck was for only $500. Your reaction probably isn't going to be one of calm and gratitude. You will most likely be angry and upset - "I thought I was getting paid $1,000, what happened? This isn't right!" Your reaction is based on your expectation of being paid one amount, and then actually getting paid a smaller amount. Similarly, when your student leaves for college and texts you only once in the first month, you might get upset or worried. Why? Because you expected they would communicate with you more often.

So BEFORE your student leaves for college, it's important to make sure everyone is on the same page by talking explicitly about how often you and your student will communicate.

I recommend keeping a similar pattern of communication as you use in high school. If you and your student talk or text frequently in high school, then you will most likely expect the same frequency in college. However, if your student is more independent and introverted, expecting a text every day may not be reasonable. It may be helpful to re-evaluate your communication plan after a few weeks. Your child's schedule and their roommate's schedule may dictate when it is the best time to talk privately. Your child may even prefer to talk with you as they walk across campus to class!

Think About It

You want to give your new college student freedom and personal space, but still want to check-in and know if they are happy and healthy on campus. Here is an example of what a communication plan can look like with your student. Feel free to add other communication topics that are important for you and your student's family situation:

- Talk about how often you will communicate with each other. Let your student talk first and encourage their input. Do they have a preferred time of day? Who will initiate contact?

- What method of communication will you use: Phone call? FaceTime®/Skype® phone call? Text? Email? Other? If you aren't comfortable using a virtual call have your student teach you how to use it before they leave for college. Sometimes your student may want to hear your voice and see your face – other times a text is sufficient to let you know they are doing okay.

Family Tip #8

When your student calls with bad news, take care of them first; then take care of yourself.

It will happen eventually – you will get a text from your student with bad news. It might not even be a message from your student that alerts you. It could be an email or letter in the mail addressed to your student with midterm grades, or a social media post or picture that sends up your parental red flag.

Imagine the scenario….First, you react, "I can't believe this!" Second, you call your student and hear their side of the story (while trying to remain calm). Third, you and your student come up with a plan to move forward. And finally – this is the part that parents often forget – you need to take care of yourself. Taking care of yourself can be as simple as making yourself a cup of tea, going for a walk/run, or listening to enjoyable music; whatever helps you relax.

It's important to take care of yourself, because we parents can hold onto bad news, and start creating scenarios in our heads about all of the worst consequences that could happen. "My student is failing a class. What if they fail all of their classes? What if they fail the semester? What if they fail out of college? What are they going to do with their life?" The easiest way to avoid this worst-case-scenario mental minefield is to take care of yourself. Find something that makes you feel good, and helps your mind avoid the "What if…" thoughts.

Think About It

Self-care is important when your student goes to college. Here are a few examples of activities that can help you relieve stress and find joy:

- Turn on uplifting music
- Write in a gratitude journal
- Go for a walk
- Spend 30 minutes writing nice comments to other people on social media
- Spend time with a pet (yours or offer to pet-sit for a friend)
- Plan a special 1:1 time with your student the next time you see them
- Download a calming app and find your favorite sounds to listen to
- Call a friend and talk on the phone or plan a get together
- Do service for someone else
- Identify 1 item/experience you are going to savor today (hot shower, hot cup of tea, favorite movie, glass of wine, fuzzy socks, etc.)
- Do a chore that you have been putting off. and when you're finished, reward yourself

Family Tip #9

Your student will get sick while they are at college – it will be okay!

When your child calls to tell you they aren't feeling well, it can be very hard for parents whose child is living away from home. It will pull at your heart strings. You may want to drive to campus to take their temperature, bring chicken soup or deliver cold medicine and cough drops. This is understandable! From a distance, it can be hard to accurately gauge if your child has a cold, the flu, or something worse. But don't worry; there are lots of resources and staff available on campus to help a sick student. Here are a few suggestions for when you get the text, "Mom, I'm not feeling well."

First, assume your child WILL get sick at least once during their first year at college. College students are notorious for spreading germs…and quickly. Resist the urge to overreact. Students who develop a runny nose from the common cold may call home claiming they have the flu. Always ask about their symptoms, and then offer treatment advice using your parental instincts. Assure your child that they will feel better soon. Next, encourage them to go to the Health & Wellness Office on campus if it is open.

If your child becomes sick in the evening or on a weekend, help them judge if their symptoms are mild enough to wait until the Health and Wellness Office opens. If not, advise them to visit an off-campus urgent care center. Of course, for severe illnesses, calling 911 is always an option.

Once your child is on the road to recovery, tell them how proud you are of them for taking care of themselves away from home! Then encourage them to contact their instructors to obtain any assignments or class notes they may have missed. It's important for them to realize that sick days in college are not free passes to avoid academic work. Finally, give yourself a pat on the back for surviving your child's illness!

Parent Story

Ann is the mom of a college freshman. Ann receives a text one night from her son and the text reads "Mom, I have the flu." Ann immediately calls her son who doesn't answer his phone. Ann texts her son and asks him to call her ASAP. While she is waiting for his phone call, Ann starts imagining all of the possible scenarios that could happen if her son has the flu…he gets sick all alone in his dorm room, he becomes dehydrated from the flu because he doesn't know to drink fluids, he is in his room alone and no one on campus knows he is there, his flu gets worse and he needs to go to the emergency room, he misses his classes and ends up failing the semester!!

Ann's son calls her 30 minutes later and Ann asks him to tell her what he is feeling, what are his symptoms, etc. Her son says that he has aches and pains all over his body, his head is throbbing, and he can't breathe through his nose. Ann asks if he feels nauseous and he says no, but his roommate had a cold last week and had the same symptoms as he does. Ann breathes a sigh of relief. "So your roommate had a cold last week?" she asks. "It sounds like you have a cold too. Stay in bed, drink lots of liquids, and take some medicine. I think you will feel better in a few days. Call me tonight."

Ann's son had incorrectly reported to his mom that he had the flu. She believed him and started down the road of thinking about all of the horrible scenarios that could happen - but would not happen because it turned out her son did NOT have the flu – he had a cold. (More in Family Tip #8)

Family Tip #10

Expect your student to make mistakes.

Expectations shape our attitudes and reactions. If we expect our children to be perfect, we will often be disappointed. If we expect some bumps in the road, we won't be surprised when we encounter a pothole.

For example, when your child first attempted to ride a bike, did you expect them to sit on the bike for the first time and ride into the sunset? Of course not! If your child sat on a bicycle seat for the first time and rode perfectly down the road, you would be amazed! We expect our children to need practice to master a skill like riding a bike. We don't expect perfection on the first try.

Likewise, when our children go off to college, they need to learn how to balance their academic demands, social demands, personal hygiene, friendships, nutrition, exercise, mental health, money management, and more, without mom or dad there to help. Like riding a bike for the first time, we can't expect them to be perfect. We should expect them to make mistakes.

When your student oversleeps for a class one day, or forgets to take their medication one day, you need to remember that your child is trying the best they can. If these occasional slip-ups become frequent, then your student might have a different issue that requires conversations and further investigation.

Think About It

Like all learning, practice and making mistakes is part of the learning curve. For example, learning how to play a musical instrument is a wonderful skill that builds confidence and is learned under the guidance of a music teacher. But learning a new instrument requires making mistakes in order to progress. College is meant to be a new learning environment and mistakes are part of the learning process.

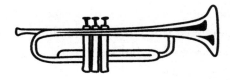

Family Tip #11

Make sure your student can make online purchases (for example, Amazon®).

Is your student able to place an order on Amazon®, or order a textbook online? Does your student know how to access their bank account online? If the answer to either of these questions is no, then you know exactly where to begin with your child this week. The ability to use a debit or credit card to make online purchases is an important skill for college students. This skill is similar to Family Tip #6, but is more focused on helping your student learn how to navigate the many payment screens encountered when making an online purchase. This may be second nature to you, but buying items online may not be intuitive for your student.

Making online purchases requires careful reading of all billing, payment, shipping, and confirmation screens. I have worked with many students who had trouble ordering their own textbooks online. In one case, the student thought they filled in every entry required to place an order. As they waited for the textbooks (that never arrived), the parents discovered the order was not completed because the credit card's security code was not properly entered! As a result of the unsuccessful online order, the student fell behind in reading and writing assignments in their courses.

There is a great teaching method called, "I DO, WE DO, YOU DO". The method is based on the gradual release of responsibility as developed by Doug Fisher and Nancy Frey. First, show your student how to make an online purchase by making a purchase yourself, making sure to discuss each step –

especially the confirmation step. Then, make an online purchase together. Finally, have your student make an online purchase independently. Good luck!

Parent Story

A.J.'s parents wanted him to buy his textbooks online and pay for them with money they deposited in his bank account. A.J. had trouble finding the textbook because there were so many versions, but he finally found it and added it to his "cart." Then he entered his credit card information and clicked Submit to finish the ordering process. A.J. waited 2 weeks and his textbook order still had not arrived. He was falling behind in class because he couldn't do the required textbook reading. A.J.'s parents asked him to look through his email account for a confirmation email of his order. A.J. looked through his inbox and found an email that said he did not enter the 3 digit security code on the card correctly and his order had not been processed!

In addition to teaching your student how to make online purchases, teach them the process and what to look for afterwards when companies confirm an online order. For example, discuss that they should receive confirmation of the order, notification when the order is shipped, and how to check the order's shipping status.

Family Tip #12

Your first visit to campus may not meet your expectations.

Whether your first visit to campus is after the first two weeks of the fall semester, Columbus Day weekend, or a college-sponsored family weekend, your visit may feel strange and confusing. The child you once knew is changing; becoming more independent. Your student will have new daily routines that are different from their routines at home. They may introduce you to their new friends, or they may not want you to meet them at all. They may want to spend every minute with you, or they may not want to spend any time with you. The changes in your child may surprise or concern you, but trust me, these changes are completely normal.

Try to manage your expectations. Expect to see dirty clothes on the dorm room floor, shaggy uncut hair, and piles of pizza boxes in their garbage can. Expecting your child to have matured and grown significantly during the first few weeks of the freshman fall semester can lead to a difficult and frustrating visit for both parents and students. Remember, your expectations affect your experience (more in Family Tip #10). If you expect your student to have miraculously learned how to do laundry, fold clothes and put them away in dresser drawers, you may be very disappointed.

Remember, your student has been creating new routines and friendships since being away at college. You may notice changes in your student's clothing, hair style/color, and mannerisms since being away at college. They may have gained weight; some students explore their new freedom by indulging in UberEats®

deliveries and late night snacks. They may feel apprehensive about your visit, anticipating that you will judge their new lifestyle, new friends, or new appearance. I encourage parents to avoid criticizing unpleasant changes in your student; instead, comment on noticeable changes in neutral or positive terms.

Before you arrive, talk with your student about your expectations. For instance, you might say, "When we arrive, I would like you to have lunch and dinner with our family, but you can spend time with your friends in between."

I encourage you to attend parent events that might be held during your visit to campus. Finding other parents who are going through the same experience can help you put your own experience with your new college student into perspective – and might even help you laugh about it.

When you are visiting your student, try to celebrate them, and find time to have a good time – to just "be" with them (more in Family Tip #18). Your student may be relieved to hear that you don't want to spend every minute of your visit with them, and that you will be attending other events on campus.

Family Tip #13

Attend the college-sponsored Family Weekend.

Halfway through the fall semester, most colleges host a Family Weekend. The main purpose of the family weekend is to welcome families to campus for a visit with their students. I strongly recommend attending this event if possible. You will learn much about how your student is handling the transition to college.

You will get to see how clean your student's dorm room is, and might meet their roommate. You will likely meet some of your student's new friends, and possibly their parents. You will get to observe your student interacting with friends, and hear the types of topics they talk about.

If possible, invite your student and a friend or two out to lunch or dinner. You will learn answers to a lot of questions you are wondering about, like, "How are your classes going? What goes on during the weekends? Who are your friends, and are they positive influences? Do you have a boyfriend/girlfriend?"

While Family Weekend is primarily meant to promote a visit with your student, college administrators often attend the weekend events, too. You may be able to sneak in a quick question or two with an administrator, but don't expect an in-depth conversation about your child's progress. This is a social weekend - have fun!

"I hold this to be the highest task for a bond between two people: that each protects the solitude of the other."

-Rainer Maria Rilke

Family Tip #14

Be patient. Your student will figure it out.

Going to college will test your student's ability to find their way in a brand new environment. They will have to adjust to a new academic, social, and residential life. They will be responsible for their own time management, eating meals in the dining hall, money management, getting enough sleep, living with a roommate, and caring for their own mental health. Wow!

Sometimes, parents expect growth to occur all at once, with equal success in all areas. Not going to happen! More likely, your new college student will quickly and easily adjust to some areas of college life, need more time to make other adjustments, and struggle for quite a while to make the remaining adjustments. This is okay.

Your student will not grow equally in all areas of college life overnight. It's simply not possible. So remember to be patient, and be thankful for the incremental growth and successes – even if it's remembering to shower every day. (Trust me, another parent is wishing their student would remember to do that!).

Remember that college success is a process. Be patient while your student learns how to put all of the pieces together.

Parent Story

Be prepared for situations like those below to happen during your student's first year at college. How do you think you will respond? How can you respond with patience?

Mya is a student who earned very good grades in high school and has excellent discipline to do homework every night. However, during the first month of college you notice pictures on her social media accounts of Mya doing everything but studying... on car rides, laughing with new friends, at events with many other students (it looks like she's at parties)! How can you react with patience?

Dan was woken up every morning in high school by his dad who also drove him to school. During Dan's first week at college he oversleeps for two classes. His dad gets upset that he doesn't use an alarm to wake up (although Dan did wake up to attend 6 out of 8 classes). He is going to the dining hall to eat meals, showering daily and getting along with his roommate. How would you react?

Kyle is a college freshman who had only a few friends in high school. He is shy and has trouble meeting new people so he prefers to play video games and talk to friends online while he plays. During the first few weeks of the semester Kyle's parents ask how he is getting along with his roommate. Kyle says his relationship with his roommate is fine and that his roommate doesn't spend much time in their dorm room. Kyle attends his classes and says they are going okay and he is doing his homework. He said he chooses to spend time in his room and play video games when he is not in class. How would you react?

Family Tip #15

Be prepared for a chaotic move-in day.

Move-in day will be crazy, no matter how much you prepare, pack, or plan. (Trust me!) Even if you have all of your student's belongings packed, dorm room furniture and matching bedspread ready to go, and tubs of macaroni and cheese in the car, something will not go according to plan.

And there's the rollercoaster of emotions being felt by you, your spouse, and your new college student. As you hold on for a wild ride, try to keep your perspective. Take pictures of your student in their new dorm room (even if your student rolls their eyes). Let them make decisions about how to set up their room, where to hang pictures, etc. The day will be crazy and emotional, but you and your student will get through it!

Think About It

Some additional words of advice for move-in day:

Bring water, it will get hot.

Remember to sit down. Bring a camping chair if there's room.

Inspect the room for damage before you move in boxes. If there is damage, bring it to the attention of the Resident Assistant.

Inquire about moving (raising or lowering) bunk beds before you do it. Some colleges allow you to do this yourself while others require that a Maintenance or Facilities department do this.

When you enter the room make sure basic room items work: the light switch, door knob locks, window shades go up and down, the window opens, closet door closes, etc. Sometimes these basics get overlooked during summer room inspections.

Talk to other parents. You will see families in the hallway, elevator, and parking lot. They are moving their student into college just like you are and can probably use a connection too. They may even live in the same state or nearby and can help you out by bringing items to campus or carpooling for rides home over the holidays. You never know. This is an opportunity to talk to other parents who are in the same situation as you are.

Family Tip #16

Make organizational tools visible in your student's dorm room.

Once you have helped your student improve their executive functioning skills at home (see Family Tip #21), you will be ready to help set up their dorm room. When helping your student move into their dorm room, be sure to put executive functioning tools in easy-to-see locations. Label totes and bins with their contents (for example: Cleaning, Personal Care, Towels/Sheets, etc.). Labels help your student become, and remain, organized. The back side of the dorm room door is a great location for a weekly calendar or white board. Place clocks and alarms near the bed (clocks with silent sweep second hands are best). Place a white board or bulletin board near your student's desk for important papers to be hung. Use the most prominent wall space for visual tools, like calendars and clocks. To the extent possible, use the same executive functioning tools that worked at home in your student's dorm room.

"Failure is so important. We speak about success all the time. But it is the ability to resist or use failure that often leads to greater success."

-J. K. Rowling

Family Tip #17

The accommodations process requires YOUR STUDENT to self-advocate.

College students with a diagnosed disability (who choose to disclose their disability) can receive accommodations from the campus Accessibility Office. This office will ask for documentation of your student's disability, and review any supporting documents your student provides (such as evaluations from a teacher, psychologist, therapist, or doctor). The Accessibility Office will determine which accommodations your student is eligible for based on the documentation they provide.

The good news is that colleges are required by law to provide "reasonable accommodations" to eligible students. Some of these accommodations may include extended time for exams, a distraction-reduced environment, use of a computer for written exams, use of a calculator, and use of text-to-speech and speech-to-text software. Other types of accommodations may include a first floor room, keypad door handles, residence hall with an elevator, etc.

Colleges are not required to follow your student's high school Individualized Education Plan, or IEP, in determining accommodations, although they may use the IEP as a guide. For instance, in high school your student may have been given a word bank for exams to help them with working memory challenges. In college, a word bank is usually not considered to be a reasonable accommodation.

It's likely that the person reviewing your student's case will want to meet with your student to discuss which accommodations YOUR STUDENT believes are necessary for their academic success. It's essential to prepare your student for this meeting (more in StudentTips #26 and #27). Even though YOU probably advocated for your student through the IEP and accommodation process in high school, YOUR STUDENT will need to advocate for themselves in college – even with the Accessibility Office.

Before leaving for college, make sure your student can answer the following three questions:

1. What is your disability (if they have one)?
2. How does your disability affect you in academic and residential settings?
3. What high school accommodations were helpful to you?

Also, make sure your student can communicate this information to someone who doesn't know them. I recommend role playing a scenario where your student is talking to a professor, or a staff member in the Accessibility Office. Your student should be able to clearly explain how their disability causes them difficulties, and which tools, strategies, or accommodations can help them be successful in college.

Family Tip #18

When your student comes home on breaks, have fun! Celebrate being with them!

Whether it happens over Labor Day weekend, Columbus Day weekend, or Thanksgiving weekend, your student will look forward to coming home - a place that is familiar to them and often a place of refuge where they can let go and just be themselves. Your student sees home as a place to unwind, sleep in their own bed, eat home cooked meals (or at least not cafeteria food), and unwind from the academic and social pressures of college. Coming home is a vacation for your child and you may see this visit home as a time to set your own plans for your child - medical appts., serious conversations about next steps, time spent looking for a part-time job, etc.

When your student comes home from college, plan something special to do with just them (such as a special dinner, or a movie you know they want to see). Celebrate your student being home – even if there are serious topics you want to talk about (such as grades, how much money they are spending, social media posts at all hours of the night, a new relationship, etc.). Make sure your student feels special when they come home, and loved!

Parent Story

Maria's daughter, Lauren, had been at school for the entire month of September and was looking forward to coming home over Columbus Day weekend. Lauren was looking forward to her mom's cooking, sleeping in on Saturday and Sunday morning, and seeing a friend from high school who was also home from college over Columbus Day weekend.

Maria was also excited to have her daughter come home. Since this was the first time Lauren had been home since move-in day, Maria had a busy weekend planned with a trip to see Lauren's grandparents who were eager to see her, a haircut appointment Saturday afternoon, the family was going to watch Lauren's younger sister play a high school soccer game, and then the family was going to a family friends' Bat Mitzvah that had been scheduled for that weekend also. Maria also wanted to have time to ask Lauren about how her classes were going, did she make any friends, etc.

Two different perspectives of what "being home" means. Even if there are "must dos" during your student's visit home be sure to incorporate some time just to enjoy them. Here are a few simple suggestions:

- Go for coffee/hot chocolate just you and your student
- Go for a walk together
- Go for a drive together while listening to music your student wants to listen to
- Plan to see a movie together that your student wants to see

Family Tip #19

Reinvest in yourself – devote time to your interests.

Who are you (besides a parent)? What do you like to do? What would you do if you had to spend several hours on yourself? Would you paint, go hiking, take dance lessons, join a book club, take an online class, or do volunteer work? Some parents feel that spending time on their own interests is selfish, but have you heard the expression, "It's hard to pour from an empty cup." You can't give your best to your children or spouse if you don't have fun or joy in your life.

One day, I asked the mother of a new college student what she planned to do with her free time now that her daughter was in college. She didn't know. I told her that her husband shared with me that she likes to sing, and has a beautiful voice. She said, "Yes, my daughter does like to sing." I said, "No, your husband told me YOU like to sing. Now you can look for opportunities to spend time doing what YOU like to do."

Sometimes, we parents become absorbed in our children's lives so much that we lose our own joy, or forget who we were and what our hobbies were before having children. Now is the time to think about what you enjoy, and how you will reinvest in yourself. Think about how you will use your extra free time, so when move-in day arrives you can start reinvesting in yourself!

Think About It

Think of yourself as a puzzle. Identify 4 characteristics, roles, hobbies, passions (puzzle pieces) that make up your puzzle - only 1 puzzle piece can be your role as a parent/caregiver for your student. While your student is at college use this time to reinvest in the other 3 puzzle pieces of your life.

Family Tip #20

Talk to your student about medications and refills.

This tip is important if your student takes any type of medication -- for any reason. Conversations about medication are important for so many reasons. Yes, it is important for your child to know the type and amount of medication they need to take each day, but it is also important for them to know HOW the medication will help them or affect them in college.

Before leaving for college, your student should be able to answer the following three questions:

1. What is the name and dosage of your medications?
2. How often do you take your medications?
3. Why is it important to take this medication?

If you are like most parents, you keep track of your student's medications and vitamins. Although this is something that is probably easiest for your family routine and for you, I encourage you to start transitioning your student's medication management to them.

Your student should know how many pills they take each day, the dosage, and how each type of medication affects them. Have conversations with your child about the times of day they take medication and talk about what to do if they oversleep and miss a dose.

You should also discuss refills. Do you want your student to notify you when the medication bottle is empty, or one, two, or three weeks before? Do you want your student to carry medications in their backpack, or keep them in their dorm room? College staff cannot dispense medications, so it's very important to have your student responsible for their own medication management BEFORE they leave for college.

Parent Story

Kiara is a college freshman who had a seizure disorder when she was in middle school. Kiara has not had any seizures in the last 4 years of high school. Kiara's seizures were usually caused by excessive heat, exercise, or not getting enough sleep. Kiara doesn't want to tell her roommate about her seizure disorder because she hadn't had any seizures recently and she doesn't want to be known as the "sick girl." One night in September, Kiara has a seizure in her dorm room while she and her roommate are hanging out. Her roommate isn't sure how to react or what to do. Kiara has not mentioned anything about her medical condition.

Another Tip: If your student has any type of medical condition, it's helpful to have a written protocol of what to do in case they are sick, have a medical episode, need help, etc. The visual directions will help both your student, their roommate or campus staff in the event of a medical emergency.

Rachel is a college freshman who has ADD (Attention Deficit Disorder). She takes prescription medication 2x day to help her focus on days when she has class. She also takes vitamins and iron supplements. Rachel chooses to fill her pill packs on Sunday afternoons for the coming week. One Sunday Rachel has her pill pack organizer and bottles of medication open and accidentally knocks them over and they fall onto the floor. Rachel is flustered and in a panic because she isn't sure that she is putting the right pills into the correct bottles / pill packs for the week.

Another Tip: If your student takes medication to control a medical issue it may be helpful to have a visual picture and description of the name of the pills he/she takes, the dosage, and frequency in your student's dorm room. The visual list can be helpful if you decide that your student is responsible for refilling medication or in the event of pills falling on the floor. Trust me, this can happen!

"Many a calm river begins as a turbulent waterfall, yet none hurtles and foams all the way to the sea."

-Mikhail Lermontov

Family Tip #21

You will receive less communication about your student's progress in college than in high school.

Parents are in the driver's seat and have significant control over their student's education while they are in high school. In college, your student becomes the driver, while parents are moved to the back seat. It's a hard transition for some parents. College administrators, advisors, and professors will communicate with your student before (and if) they will communicate with the parents. This can seem crazy, especially if the parents are helping to finance their student's college education. There is a privacy law in higher education, called the Family Educational Rights and Protection Act, or FERPA. This law prohibits college staff from communicating with you about your student, because your child is 18 years old and legally an adult, unless your student waives their right of privacy.

Because your new college student is (in most cases) at least 18 years old, they are legally an adult. Therefore, all mail and electronic communication from the college is required to go directly to them. Likewise, your student will be the primary recipient of financial aid information, college bills, health information, disability-related information, academic calendars, residential move in/out dates, etc.

Colleges formally update students on their academic progress twice each semester by issuing midterm and final grades. These academic updates are sent by mail and posted online. Therefore, parents can ask their students to send them copies of their midterm and final grades each semester. Minimized communication in college is one of the most difficult transitions for parents who are accustomed to being in the driver's seat for their student's education. College's know this, but hold firm to FERPA laws of privacy. This tip has no sugarcoating – it is what it is.

Think About It

Before strating college talk to your child about the Family Educational Rights and Protection Act (FERPA), what it is, and what it means. Decide together if they will sign a release so that you can communicate with the college directly. If together you decide that they will not sign the relase, talk about the importance of them forwarding to you all emails regarding tuition payments, insurance, move-in / move-out dates, etc.

Family Tip #22

Give yourself time to adjust to your child being away at college.

Family Tip #14 encourages you to approach your child's transition to college with patience. The same advice applies to you, too. There's no question that your child's college journey has affected your life, and your family's dynamic, in a big way. Allow yourself to feel your feelings. Treat yourself with patience and compassion. Be easy with yourself and allow yourself to feel whatever it is you feel in the moment. Your feelings may change from moment to moment, and you may experience more than one feeling at the same time! That's okay. Be patient with yourself.

There is no rush to "have it all together" once your child goes to college. If you feel like texting your daughter and telling her, "I love you," do it. If you feel like sending your son a message that says, "I'm proud of you," do it. They may need to read your words of encouragement as much as you need to send them. Above all, try to enjoy this new phase in your child's life – and in your life! And be patient with yourself.

"Laughter is an instant vacation."

-Milton Berle

Family Tip #23

Ask about the support systems at your student's college. Who should they contact for help and how do they identify when help is needed?

As mentioned in Family Tip #17, one of the biggest differences between high school and college is the need for your student to be a self-advocate and seek help when help is needed. In college, no news is good news, so the college staff will assume that everything is going well with your student unless they speak up when they need something.

I suggest that parents identify the college's support systems as soon as possible. You can request this information during an open house, while on a college tour, or even on move-in day. You should know the college person, office, or department your student can reach out to when they need help.

Typically, the college academic advisor will be the primary point of contact if your student has academic-related difficulties or questions. If residence life issues arise (such as roommate problems, laundry issues, and dorm room maintenance issues), your student would contact someone on the Residence Life staff – most likely the Resident Assistant. Lastly, if your student is having challenges that are related to their disability, the Accessibility Office should be contacted. You are a caring parent and want to know what safety nets are in place on campus to help your child. But remember, it will be your student who needs to self-advocate and use these support systems.

Think About It

Here are a few suggested questions to ask to help your student (and you) identify the support systems on your child's college campus.

Academic Concerns
Who is their Academic Advisor?
Who is the Director of Advising?

Disability Concerns
Who is the Director of Accessibility Office?
Are there other Accessibility Specialists in the Accessibility Office?
Are there Learning Specialists or fee based academic supports?

Residential Life
Who is their Resident Assistant (RA)?
Who is their Resident Director (RD)?
Who is the Director of Residence Life?

Health Concerns
What is the name of the Counselor(s) on campus?
What is the name of the Nurse / Doctor on campus?

Family Tip #24

Colleges communicate with students, not parents.

A big difference between high school and college is that academics in college will largely be the responsibility of your student. Your student will have access to their grades via a campus portal/website; your student will contact their professors if they have a question; your student will need to seek tutoring support or academic accommodations if they are needed. ALL of the academic information in your student's college journey will be managed by them.

Because your student is most likely at least 18 years of age, colleges and universities (under the rules of FERPA) view your student as an adult, and will communicate only with them, unless your student signs a form that permits the college to release information to specified individuals. Even when this form is signed, the amount of information shared between a college and a parent is limited – not to hide information from parents, but to transfer the educational responsibility from the parent to the student. I recommend that your student seek answers to academic questions themselves, with the parents offering guidance (in the background) if needed.

Think About It

Here are a few resources that campuses offer to help parents stay informed about campus events and important dates (while not taking away their student's independence):

- Find out about social activities on campus by following the college's social media accounts (more in Student Tip # 1).

- Attend Family Weekend in the fall (more in Family Tip #13). Talk to other families and ask if there are ways that they stay updated on events or how they encourage their student to advocate for themselves.

- Does your college have a Parent and Families Office? If so, ask if the office prints parent newsletters or sends emails with resources and information for families.

- Look on the college's website for the academic and semester calendars. The calendars will inform you when midterm grades and final grades are submitted by faculty, when classes are cancelled due to holidays, move-in and move-out dates at the beginning and end of the semesters, etc.

Family Tip #25

Help your student do what they don't want to do.

As adults, we know that sometimes we have to do tasks we don't want to do. Tax forms must be filed every year whether we want to or not. The trash needs to be emptied regularly whether it's raining, snowing, or sunny outside. Likewise, college students need to attend appointments and have conversations they would prefer to avoid. These difficult conversations might include talking to their roommate about privacy issues, addressing something a roommate said that was mean or hurtful, talking to a professor when your student is struggling in a class, or talking to a coach about an issue with a teammate.

In college, there are appointments and conversations that are inevitable. It can be tempting to help your student avoid these difficult situations by solving the problem yourself, but don't. Instead, assure them that they CAN and WILL make it through the difficult situation and you have faith in them.

Remind them of a past experience when they demonstrated _____. (Insert a quality your student demonstrated – compassion, dedication, kindness, courage, passion, persistence, etc.) Life is full of difficult situations, so families need to equip their students with the tools to work through challenging times; to have confidence in themselves and their ability to persevere; and to stand in the storm with faith that it will pass.

"Maybe I can't stop the downpour,
but I will always join you
for a walk in the rain."

-Unknown

Bonus Family Tip

Be prepared for an emotional rollercoaster ride when your student returns home from college on a break.

College students are eager to return home on breaks. But when they do, they aren't completely home. Being home gives your student a sense of comfort and familiarity, but their routines and relationships with family members will be different when they get home. You see, they have grown more independent since leaving for college. The college student that returns home will not be the same child that left for college.

When your student returns home, they may expect you to recognize and respect that they have grown more independent. Rather than spending time at home, your student may rush out the door to reconnect with high school friends. They might bicker with siblings, stay up late, question old family habits/routines, and seemingly sleep all day. When your child returns home over breaks, they will be redefining their role in the family. This is normal.

Your student may have made new friends at college, or connected with new peer groups who dress and speak differently than their high school friends. You may notice changes in your student's clothing, hair style/color, speech, etc. I encourage parents to comment on noticeable changes in neutral or positive ways.

As you become aware of the changes in your student, your feelings toward them may alternate between love, tension, sadness, and confusion until you and your student settle into a newly defined relationship. You will find a new normal, that works for both of you. Be patient and understanding as you renegotiate family expectations and relationships.

"Don't worry about a thing 'cause every little thing is gonna be all right."

-Bob Marley

Acknowledgements

This book was inspired by the stories, laughter, tears and relationships I have had the privilege to share with countless families who entrusted me with their children as a teacher, learning specialist or life coach in college. Your stories fueled my passion and what I feel is my calling.

Thank you to my family for offering me support and space when I was busy pursuing my passion. My dad's red pen, both literal and virtual, helped when I was younger and in the writing of this book. Thank you to my mom who encouraged me with positive words, love and teaching me how to help others. Thank you to my sister for your strength and advice - Sasha Fierce!

Many people were instrumental in the publishing of this book; Cindy Samul, for your amazing cover design and book design. Your talent brought my words and vision to life in a beautiful way. Thank you to Susan Yellin, Tammy Byron, Jackie Connell, Marydee Sklar, Paul Magoulis and Barbara Kipfer, and many others who offered feedback about the book. Lois, thank you for 'getting me' and knowing that inspiration is at the heart of everything I do.

Last and not least, I dedicate this book to Lana, Emily and Ron. Lana and Emily - you are the reason my heart is so big. You both are beautiful examples of kindess and light. I love you. Finally to my husband, Ron. You are the reason this book is written. You see in me words and a vision that need to be shared. Your words and love inspire my words and love. This book would only be ideas in my head without your support and AIS philosophy.

About the Author

Jennifer Sullivan is a veteran educator with experience in both higher education and K-12 settings supporting students and parents in the transition to college. She discovered her passion for working with families of students with disabilities in 2006 as a founding faculty member of a college transition program in New England. She is an educator, speaker, and writer who has published many articles on the topics of technology use in the classroom, student engagement, and educational equity. Her work has appeared in ADDitude Magazine, Edutopia, Collegiate Parent, Grown and Flown, Faculty Focus and many others. She has presented nationally for the Learning Disabilities Association of America (LDA), CT Secondary Transition Symposium, and Independent Educational Consultants Association (IECA). She lives on the shore of southeastern Connecticut with her husband and two daughters.

For More Tips, Checklists, and Transition to College Resources for Students and Families Scan This QR Code.

Made in the USA
Middletown, DE
28 April 2021